Always a Bridesmaid....

A Survival Guide for the Bridal Party

by
Tabitha Wilkins Olzinski

authorHOUSE™

1663 LIBERTY DRIVE, SUITE 200
BLOOMINGTON, INDIANA 47403
(800) 839-8640
WWW.AUTHORHOUSE.COM

First published by AuthorHouse 07/29/05

ISBN: 1-4208-5602-2 (sc)

Library of Congress Control Number: 2005904486

Printed in the United States of America
Bloomington, Indiana

This book is printed on acid-free paper.

This book is dedicated to my husband, Brian, for all of his love and support, to my parents for always being there unconditionally, and to my girlfriends who are married, engaged, or single.

Table of Contents

Chapter I
Where to begin?

———◦———

*T*he phone rings unexpectedly early one morning. Quickly you reach for it, not quite awake.

"Hello?" you say in a mumble.

It is a long-time girlfriend on the other end.

"Guess what?", she gasps.

"What?", you question.

"_____ asked me to marry him last night!!!", she says excitedly.

Now wide awake, you both express excitement over her revelation. The next half hour is spent listening to her telling you about the entire event, from the way he asked her, to her reaction, to what the ring looks like. And then she asks the question.

"I want to ask you to be in the wedding?" she says hopefully.

"Really?," you reply, then add, "Of course, I'd love to!"

You hang up the phone only to switch from elation to panic-stricken. "Now what do I do? Where do I start?," you think, "I don't know what I need to do to be in a wedding!"

This book is designed to help you from this point on. By the end of this book, you should feel that you have all the answers you need to confidently carry out your duties as a member of the bridal party.

So let's begin!

Let's start with your title.

MAID OF HONOR

This is an *unmarried* woman who agrees to stand for the bride at the wedding ceremony and is in essence "the head bridesmaid." This person will also sign the marriage certificate as a witness to the marriage.

MATRON OF HONOR

This is a *married* woman who agrees to stand for the bride at the wedding ceremony and is seen as "the head bridesmatron." This person will also sign the marriage certificate as a witness to the marriage.

BRIDESMAID

This is an *unmarried* woman who stands for the bride behind the maid of honor at the wedding ceremony.

BRIDESMATRON

This is a *married* woman who stands for the bride behind the matron of honor (or maid of honor if there is not a matron of honor) at the wedding ceremony.

JUNIOR BRIDESMAID

This is an *unmarried* girl who is under sixteen, but is also part of the bridal party as a bridesmaid.

FLOWER GIRL

This is a little girl, usually about the age of five or six, who walks down the aisle before the bride to sprinkle flower petals. Due to age, the flower girl may or may not stand during the ceremony.

RING BEARER

This is a little boy, usually between the ages of five and ten, who carries the bride and groom's rings down the aisle on a pillow.

BEST MAN

This is the man picked by the groom to stand by him as a witness during the wedding ceremony and is seen as the "head groomsman." This person will also sign the marriage certificate as a witness to the marriage.

GROOMSMEN

These are the men, married or single, who stand for the groom during the ceremony behind the best man.

USHERS

These are the men who seat the guests before the wedding ceremony. They can be the same people chosen as groomsmen or different.

Chapter II
What do I need to do first?

———⟫·◦·⟪———

O nce you find your place in the bridal party you can begin to fulfill your obligations in this role. However, no matter where you fall in the bridal party your first obligation comes as soon as the couple announces their engagement.

Some couples will have an engagement party, which is where the bride and groom's families announce the couples' engagement formally to family and friends. If the couple has an engagement party it is appropriate to bring a gift to celebrate the occasion. However, if the couple does not have this formal event it is also proper to give the couple a gift to begin their celebration.

Appropriate gifts are anything related to the upcoming wedding. Inexpensive, but very helpful and thoughtful, are subscriptions to bridal magazines ($10-$15 for a year's subscription) and bridal book planners found at your local bookstore ($15-$30). If the bride has a computer, wedding planning computer programs are now available at local computer stores for around $30. (However, before this purchase, make sure you find out the type of computer the bride has so as to get the correct software.) If you want to get the couple a gift more personalized to them, such as a dinner gift certificate to their favorite restaurant, use your creativity, but a $30-$35 limit should apply.

Your next task should be to make a list of all the bridesmaid's/matron's addresses and phone numbers so they can all contact each other for further correspondence. This will also help the bride out along the way.

This task should be reserved for the matrons/maids of honor, but any bridesmaid should feel free to perform this task if the matrons/maids of honor fail to do so. Most weddings have an average of 3-6 bridesmaids/matrons, but weddings in the South have been known to have 11-12. Please copy the information on the following pages and forward one copy to each member of the bridal party.

MAID OF HONOR:

Name:_____

Address:_____

_____

_____

e-mail _____

Phone: hm.(_____)_____

Wk/cell(_____)_____

MATRON OF HONOR:

Name:_____

Address:_____

_____

_____

e-mail _____

Phone: hm.(_____)_____

Wk/cell(_____)_____

BRIDESMAIDS and BRIDESMATRONS:

Name:_____

Address:_____

_____

_____

e-mail _____

Phone: hm.(_____)_____

Wk/cell(_____)_____

Name:_____

Address:_____

_____

_____

e-mail _____

Phone: hm.(_____)_____

Wk/cell(_____)_____

Name:_____

Address:_____

_____

_____

e-mail _____

Phone: hm.(_____)_____

Wk/cell(_____)_____

Name:_____

Address:_____

_____

_____

e-mail _____

Phone: hm.(_____)_____

Wk/cell(_____)_____

Name:_____

Address:_____

_____

_____

e-mail _____

Phone: hm.(_____)_____

Wk/cell(_____)_____

Name:_____

Address:_____

_____

_____

e-mail _____

Phone: hm.(_____)_____

Wk/cell(_____)_____

Name:_____

Address:_____

_____

_____

e-mail _____

Phone: hm.(_____)_____

Wk/cell(_____)_____

Name:_____

Address:_____

_____

_____

e-mail _____

Phone: hm.(_____)_____

Wk/cell(_____)_____

Name:_____

Address:_____

_____

_____

e-mail _____

Phone: hm.(_____)_____

Wk/cell(_____)_____

Name:_____

Address:_____

_____

_____

e-mail _____

Phone: hm.(_____)_____

Wk/cell(_____)_____

JUNIOR BRIDESMAIDS:

Name:_____

Address:_____

_____

_____

e-mail _____

Phone:(_____)_____

Name:_____

Address:_____

_____

_____

e-mail _____

Phone:(_____)_____

Tabitha Wilkins Olzinski

Name:_____

Address:_____

_____

_____

e-mail _____

Phone:(_____)_____

Chapter III
What does the bride have to do?

*T*his chapter is prepared to help you understand what the bride has to accomplish before the upcoming event. It is written so that you can know what kind of pressure the bride is under and how you can help.

First, the bride must pick who she wants to participate in the wedding. This can be an agonizing decision as some roles are more important than others and relatives and friends can have preconceived expectations.

The list of those in the wedding includes: all of her bridesmaids/matrons, a maid or matron of honor or both, junior bridesmaids (optional), flower girl (optional), and ring bearer (optional). She must also decide if she wants to have anyone sing at the wedding, do any readings, or to handle the guest book signing.

The bride must also:

* pick a wedding date
* pick a wedding location
* decide who will perform the ceremony
* pick a photographer
* find herself a wedding dress
* find the bridesmaids/matrons dresses
* make out a guest list
* find a location for the reception
* secure a florist and pick out flowers
* choose a cake and a bakery
* pick music to be sung/played at the ceremony and reception and find the performers
* pick out and register for china, crystal, and silver patterns
* pick out and word the wedding invitations
* address/mail wedding invitations
* pick out food for the reception/hire a caterer
* have her picture formally taken by the photographer for her local newspaper
* write and submit a newspaper article announcing her engagement and one after the wedding announcing the unity

* attend couple counseling sessions with the priest or
  rabbi, if required
* have a blood test
* apply for a wedding license
* select gifts for the bridal party
* select a gift for the groom
* pick out wedding rings
* plan a honeymoon
* write thank-you notes
* apply for a name change
* find a place to live after the marriage
* help out-of-town guests/bridal party members find
  lodging
* plan a bridesmaid luncheon
* attend bridal showers
* help the groom plan the rehearsal dinner.

If the above list makes *you* dizzy, imagine how the bride
must feel, especially if she is balancing these tasks between
going to school or work.

Chapter IV
How can I help?

———⟐———

MAIDS/MATRONS OF HONOR

*B*efore the wedding ceremony you can offer to go with the bride to accomplish a lot of her tasks, for support and input. Let's go over these.

First, you can offer to help with the bridesmaid/matron dresses. Offer to look through magazines with the bride or offer to go with her to look and try on bridesmaid dresses. The maid/matron of honor sometimes wears a slightly different dress than the bridesmaids/matrons – usually the same color, but a slightly different style. Any pregnant bridesmaids/matrons can also wear a slightly different dress-some styles offer a pregnancy line, be sure to ask if there are any pregnant women in the wedding party. You can offer suggestions and give input, but remember that this is the bride's wedding! Most bridesmaid/matron dresses cost between $100-$200. This depends on the taste of the bride and the financial situations of the bridesmaids/matrons and can vary above and below this range. One thing to note is that most bridesmaid dress stores carry their dresses in junior sizes, so don't be insulted when you have to order a size ten dress and you normally wear a size eight. Also, don't forget to have pregnant bridesmaids/matrons order in a size appropriate to their stage of pregnancy during the wedding date. Some stores have pregnancy pillows to help a bridesmaid/matron make a more accurate guess. Know that most stores won't order a single dress until *all* the dress orders and deposits are in. This is done so the dresses can be made from the same dye lot minimizing color variations. Dresses usually take 2-4 months to come in after they are ordered and vary by designer and store, so start shopping early.

The shoes that go with the dress usually have to be dyed and can cost between $30-$50. Before any bridesmaids order a shoe size they need to talk to the person dying the shoes to discuss shrink ability factors. Some shoes shrink 1/2 a size as the dye dries, so it is necessary in this case to have everyone order a size 1/2 larger than normal to have them fit at the wedding.

To help get everyone through these tasks, the maid/
matron of honor can arrange a fitting party at the salon that
is ordering the final pick dresses. This requires the bridal
party to have a set appointment to go to the bridal salon
where the bridesmaid dresses have been found. The maid/
matron of honor takes on the task of calling all of the women
in the bridal party and inviting them to the fitting party. The
maid/matron of honor can then bring some water (no juice or
soda so the dresses aren't ruined with a spill) and some light
snacks for everyone to munch on during the fitting process.
This task can be done when first ordering the dresses and
also when the dresses arrive. The fitting party usually helps
to alleviate a lot of anxiety in the bride who will know that
everyone will have a dress and have it fit for her wedding.

You can also offer to go with the bride to pick out
bridesmaid/matron gifts. These gifts are usually jewelry that
the bridesmaids/matrons wear during the wedding, but they
can be more individualized depending on what the bride
would like to do. These gifts are usually given at the rehearsal
of the wedding or at a bridesmaid luncheon if the bride is
having one.

You can also accompany the bride in finding a gift for the
groom that she will give to him after the wedding ceremony,
preferably during the honeymoon.

The bride should also give a gift of thanks to her parents
or guardians as an acknowledgment of their help during the

planning of the wedding and possibly for payment of the reception. You can help her with this task as well.

Some brides would also like input on their own wedding dress. They may ask you to accompany them during this task, since most brides do not want the groom to see them in their wedding dress before the wedding day.

Another thing that maid/matrons of honor can help with is finding accommodation for out-of-town wedding guests. Help the bride by calling local hotels to get rates. Don't forget to check on a special rate that can be given if a block of rooms are reserved for the wedding guests.

Probably the biggest responsibility of the maid/matron of honor is to throw a shower for the bride to be. This can be done in collaboration with the other bridesmaids/matrons for financial reasons, but the maid/matron of honor should be in charge of the planning process.

THE BRIDAL SHOWER

This party should occur anywhere from three months to three weeks before the wedding and can take on a variety of forms. The following are a few suggestions for wedding showers.

Around the clock shower: For this shower, each guest should have a specified hour of the day on their invitation; this could be 3pm or 3am. The guest should be instructed to bring a gift that the bride can use during this hour of the day.

Many guests can be very creative with this knowledge and it also reduces the chance of having duplicate gifts.

Lingerie shower: This type of shower is best saved for a bride who doesn't easily get embarrassed. All guests are asked to bring some lingerie for the new bride to have for her honeymoon. This could get pretty risqué depending on the personality of the guests invited. For this type of shower the future bride can register at a local lingerie store for proper fit and desirable attire.

Garden/yard couple shower: More and more brides want to include their groom in the wedding shower process and the couple shower is becoming more and more popular. For this shower both men and women friends of the bride and groom are invited and asked to bring a gift *she* can use in the garden or a gift *he* can use in the yard. This idea can also be used for any other specific room in the house such as a kitchen, dining room, or living room and can be more specific such as a "stock the bar" party where all guests bring something pertaining to a bar.

The size of the shower will depend on the budget of those giving it and the guest list given by the bride. Usually the bridesmaids are not the only ones giving a shower to the bride, so the guest list should vary so as not to overwhelm the same guests. However, the bridesmaids/matrons are invited to every shower and proper protocol is to send a gift if one cannot make it to the shower. Usually the people giving the shower are exempt from giving a gift as the shower is seen as a gift, but some people do both.

Most showers last 2-3 hours and include opening of gifts, light food, and possibly some game playing. An example of a game may be asking guests to find as many words as they can out of the bride and groom's full name, or unscrambling words you have disguised that pertain to the wedding (e.g. diabrmdeis = bridesmaid).

Small prizes are sometimes given to the winners, such as a candy bar or a wedding garter.

This is also an opportunity to find out more about the bride from her friends and family as the people a bride invites to her shower are usually those closest to her. Here is another fun idea: Pass around a roll of toilet paper or a bag of candy. Tell each guest to take as much as they like and hold it. After everyone is done, ask each guest to tell one thing about the bride for each square of toilet paper or each piece of candy they have taken.

During the gift opening, one person should write down what each gift is and whom it is from. This helps the bride with her thank-you notes after the shower. Also, during the gift opening process, someone usually uses the bows from the gifts to attach them to paper plates. These will serve as mock bouquets for the bride and bridesmaids to carry during the rehearsal of the wedding when the real bouquets will not be available. Finally, someone should warn the bride that legend has it that for each ribbon/bow the bride tears she and the groom can expect a child!

After the wedding showers are over you can take a few days to breathe easy until the rest of the wedding festivities begin.

The following is a layout to help you organize your wedding shower! You should give yourself at least a month before the wedding shower to plan and organize!

HOST/HOSTESS:_____
_____

DATE:___/___/_____
TIME:_____until _____
LOCATION:_____

PEOPLE TO INVITE:

NAME	ADDRESS	RSVP

NAME	ADDRESS	RSVP

Use the following as a checklist to make sure you aren't left with last-minute things undone!

THINGS TO DO FOUR WEEKS BEFORE THE SHOWER:

- Meet with the bride to pick a date and time _____
- Have the bride give you a list of people to invite along with addresses _____
- Secure a location _____

THINGS TO DO THREE WEEKS BEFORE THE SHOWER:

- Buy or make shower invitations _____
Options from least expensive to most expensive:

> a. Buy a packet of pre-printed invitations from a card store and hand-write information inside.
> b. Buy printed paper from a party store and print up your own invitations on a computer.
> c. Have invitations ordered and printed at a card store.

A wedding shower invitation should include the following information:

- Who the shower is for
- The date of the shower
- The time of the shower, being sure to include a beginning and an ending time
- The location of the shower
- The type of shower/designated type of gift
- Who is giving the shower and a phone number to RSVP or to answer questions and give directions.

(It is improper to list on the invitation where the bride is registered. If they call to ask, you can tell them then.)

On the following page is an example of how a shower invitation may read.

- Buy stamps   _____
- Address and mail out invitations   _____

Please join us for an

Around the House Shower

Honoring

SUSAN SMITH

June 9th 2005

3:00pm-5:30pm

4321 Peachtree Road

Atlanta, GA

Given by: Tabitha Olzinski

Regrets only: (123)456-7890

Directions: Go south on Peachtree Road and turn left at your first light. Take your second right into our driveway.

TWO WEEKS BEFORE THE SHOWER:

- Create menu and shopping list   _____
- Create layout of order of events to happen _____

(E.g.:2:00-2:15 Guests arrive

        2:15-2:45 Guests eat

        2:45-3:30 Games are played

        3:30-4:00 Opening of gifts

        4:00-4:30 Guests mingle)

ONE WEEK TO ONE DAY BEFORE THE SHOWER:

- Shop for all food items needed   _____
- Order cake (if having one)   _____
- Buy small prizes if playing games   _____
- Buy/make items for game playing   _____

THE DAY OF THE SHOWER:

- Set up the decorations (if needed)   _____
- Make/set up food   _____
- Set up chairs/tables   _____
- Put out a notebook and pen to write down
  gifts received   _____
- Put out tape/paper plates etc to make mock
  bridal bouquets   _____
- Designate a place for gifts   _____

BRIDESMAIDS/MATRONS

Most bridesmaids can and will participate in some or all of the above. This will depend on the wishes of the bride and the availability of the bridesmaid.

In addition, bridesmaids/matrons can also offer to help with stuffing and addressing of wedding invitations.

OUT-OF-TOWN BRIDAL PARTY MEMBERS

Most commonly a bride will pick a local friend to be a maid/matron of honor, due to the high amount of responsibility, and have her out-of-town friends be bridesmaids/matrons. In this case, your availability is limited so calling the bride often to check on her mental status and needs may be the limits of your interaction. If you live close enough, you can take weekend trips to visit and help the bride with needed tasks as well as give the matrons/maids of honor a rest.

As for dresses, if you are an out-of-town bridesmaid you may not see the dress until it arrives on your doorstep. You may call or fax over your measurements to the bridal salon and they can send the dress to you. Some brides, however, may send you on an excursion to try on dresses in your town to see what you like and report back to her. You should be honest, but not brutal, as this is the bride's wedding. However, if you just cannot wear a particular dress, tactfully tell the bride this and hopefully a compromise can be reached. If a dress is very form-fitting and you are uncomfortable with wearing that style, tell the bride that you really like the dress and the color she picked out but you don't feel that this particular dress fits your body type. If she really is stuck on ordering this dress then maybe you can order a larger size and wear it a little looser. If you don't like sleeveless dresses maybe there is a shawl that comes with the dress that you can wear draped over your shoulders to make the dress more elegant.

If you are an out-of-town wedding party member be sure not to forget to begin checking airfares and local hotel rates three to six months ahead of time to get the best rates. Sometimes the bride can help find accommodation with friends or local bridal party members to cut down on costs for the out-of-town wedding party members.

JUNIOR BRIDESMAIDS/RING BEARERS/FLOWER GIRLS

Due to the ages no responsibilities usually fall on this group of the wedding party. Brides will usually find dresses/suits for this group to wear, or she may just specify a color and let the parents pick out the dresses/suits for their children.

Depending on the appropriateness, this group may or may not be invited to various showers and wedding activities.

GROOMSMEN/USHERS

This group is usually the group the bride worries about the most. Most men are last minute at getting their fittings for their tuxedos and can send the bride into a tether of anxiety.

Groomsmen need to find out the tuxedo store the wedding party is using and give their measurements at least a month in advance. Most tuxedo stores will give the groom his tuxedo for free if the entire wedding party uses the same store.

For out-of-town groomsmen, you can go to a local tuxedo store to get measured and then fax, mail, or phone in your measurements.

Groomsmen then go back the day of the wedding to pick up their tuxedos. Sometimes one groomsman is designated to pick up all of the tuxedos and bring them to the church and another is designated to make sure they are all returned. No fittings need to be made.

Other responsibilities that fall within this group are: organizing a bachelor party for the groom and seating the guests at the wedding.

SPECIAL NEEDS BRIDAL PARTY MEMBERS

If you need to have special equipment or access to events, such as wheelchair ramps, make sure that the bride or groom is sensitive to this need when picking locations for their events.

Also, make sure to call event locations yourself in plenty of time prior to the event to see if special arrangements can be made to accommodate your needs.

Finally, for all bridal party members, don't forget to get the couple a wedding gift. This can be easily forgotten during all of the other precipitance surrounding the wedding. Technically, under good manners you have a year after the wedding date to give the couple a gift.

Chapter V
A week before the wedding

———————◆◦◦◦◆———————

At this point the wedding should pretty much be in place. You should have your dress fitted by now or tuxedo ordered and everyone in the wedding party should now volunteer to help with last-minute things.

Bridal party members should get together a survival kit for the day of the wedding.

For women this should include:

• Tylenol
• Extra bobby pins/hair clips
• A few extra pairs of hosiery

- Band aids
- Nail polish
- Hair spray
- A small sewing kit/needle and thread
- Tissues
- Sewing scissors to cut threads or arm hanger straps
- Change for a vending machine.

During this weekend bridesmaids/matrons and maids/matrons of honor may be invited to a bridal luncheon. This is sometimes given by a close friend or by the bride herself. This is a thank-you to the bridal party for all of their help, so take this time to enjoy yourself. Appropriate dress is usually a nice dress or pant suit, unless otherwise specified by the bride.

Another common occurrence of the weekend before the wedding is the bachelor and bachelorette parties. Traditionally seen as taking the bride or groom out for one last night to let loose and party with their friends as singles before delving into marriagedom. Some brides and grooms, however, now elect to party together just to include all of their friends. A fun activity to do during this night is to have a scavenger hunt for the bride or groom. Make a list of items the bride or groom has to find before the night is through, such as having their picture taken with a girl named Sam, or finding a particular book or t-shirt. Having the party a week before the wedding is a good idea to allow for a complete recovery from any over-indulgence.

Finally, if the bride or groom have any pets that need to be taken care of while they are on their honeymoon, this is a good time to offer to help find someone to pet sit or to offer yourself.

Chapter VI
The day before the wedding

On this day, bridal party members should offer to escort out-of-town wedding guests/wedding party members to their hotels from the airport.

The bride may have set up appointments for the bridal party to have a hair/nail day at a local salon. If not, offer to help the bride work with her hair to decide how to wear it on the big day. Helping the bride to make sure she has everything for tomorrow is also appreciated. The bride may be leaving on a honeymoon tomorrow and may need to pack. She may need to pick up last-minute things so helping her to run errands or make last-minute confirmations will help.

THE WEDDING REHERSAL

That evening expect to attend a wedding rehearsal followed by rehearsal dinner. Usually the rehearsal starts around 6:00pm and can last for 30 minutes to 2 hours depending on the timeliness of all those needed for rehearsal and the complexity of the wedding itself. Dress for this activity depends on the bride, so ask her preference.

During this time, the bridal party will practice where to stand and how to get there. Also what actions, such as sitting, fluffing the bride's train, taking her flowers, or giving over the rings is practiced.

Usually the best man and maid/matron of honor hold onto the real wedding rings to use during the ceremony. If a ring bearer is involved he may or may not carry the actual rings. He may instead carry mock rings to account for their possible loss due to the ring bearer's age.

This is also the time to practice walking while carrying flowers. Use the mock flower arrangements made from the bows of the bridal showers. Although the bows will be lightweight as compared to the real arrangements, you can get used to carrying something while you walk down the aisle. Try to carry the flowers as you will have to carry them tomorrow. The bride may have you carry a bouquet you hold in both hands, long-stemmed flowers you would hold like a baby, or a basket of flowers that you may hold in front of you with both hands or hung on your wrist.

During the rehearsal, some brides have a superstition of not walking down the aisle until the real thing, so you may be asked to stand in her place.

Make sure you ask any questions you have about your place during this practice to avoid confusion tomorrow.

Once everyone feels satisfied about what they are to do tomorrow, the next step is to go to the rehearsal dinner. This can come in a variety of forms, although generally it is the groom and his family's responsibility. It can be a catered dinner at the family's home of the bride or groom, a casual barbecue, a potluck dinner, a dinner at a local restaurant, etc.

One warning for members of the bridal party, the rehearsal dinner is the appropriate time for the best man, maid/matron of honor and any other good-meaning family member or friend to toast the bride and groom on their future life together. Timing is up to the person performing the toast, however, before the main course is the usual. This includes telling how you know the couple and telling a story about how they are a good match, or just wishing them luck.

After the rehearsal dinner the bridal party is free to do as they want until the morning. Sometimes the bride requests the bridesmaids to spend the night with her to calm any jitters.

Chapter VII
The big day

*C*ommunication is key during this day to avoid last-minute mix-ups. Keeping the bride and groom from seeing each other until the ceremony, if this is their request, is an example of using good communication among the bridal party.

Depending on the time of the wedding, the bride may have opted to have the bridesmaid luncheon on this day. She, as well as the bridesmaids, may have appointments for make-up, hair, and nails on this day too. Just make sure your appointments allow you to be available at least two hours before the wedding.

Hours before the ceremony you should also figure out your parking and driving plan. Sometimes the wedding party is taken to the wedding site via limousine or they can be taken from the wedding site to the reception via limousine. Therefore, you should park your car at the wedding site or reception first and have someone drive you back to where you are supposed to meet the wedding party. This will keep you from being stranded without a ride home at the end of the festivities.

During this time, most bridesmaids meet together either at someone's house or at the wedding site itself to dress, help each other get ready, and help calm the bride. Be sure to bring some light snacks and drinks that are non-staining to this event. This will keep away any lightheaded feelings, since most brides and bridesmaids may have forgotten to eat during this day.

You will be given your bridal bouquet at this time so keep track of it. Some bridesmaids use their bouquet to conceal tissue for use as needed during the ceremony by wrapping it around the stem.

The groomsmen are usually more mischievous during this time and usually try to find the car the newlyweds will drive off in and decorate it without the couple's knowledge. Common non-damaging actions include writing "Just Married," the date, and the couple's name in shoe polish on the windshield, tying empty cans or old shoes to the back of the car, or filling the car with balloons.

During this time you will also be the target of many photos. Some photographers like to take candid pictures of the bridesmaids fixing each other's hair, etc. Most brides opt to take as many photographs as possible before the wedding to cut down on the time this consumes after the ceremony. Most couples take all the pictures they can think of without the bride and groom together, so as to keep the bride's appearance spectacular to the groom as she walks down the aisle.

Pictures are usually finished about 30 minutes before the start of the ceremony. This allows the groomsmen to seat guests accordingly and bridesmaids to do last-minute touch-ups.

For the groomsmen or ushers, this will be the time for you to greet and seat guests. Just remember that those on the bride's side are seated to the left and those on the groom's side are seated to the right. Also, you need to find out if there are any reserved seating for special family members or friends.

THE WEDDING CEREMONY

At about 10 minutes before the wedding most groomsmen stop seating guests. The bridesmaids and those seated in honor such as the bride and groom's parents and grandparents line up at this point. Bridesmaids are usually lined up shortest to tallest with the maid/matron of honor last. The music for the ceremony usually begins to play in the background at this time.

At the time of the wedding ceremony, now arriving guests should wait until the seating of the families before entering. The usual procession is to have the bride and groom's grandparents and then parents escorted to the front rows.

At this point, the music may change, signifying the beginning procession of the bridal party. Hold your flowers at waist height, your elbows resting on your hips. Sometimes the bridesmaids walk down the aisle alone, sometimes they are escorted down by groomsmen. This is all at the preference of the bride and groom.

The bridesmaids should have established a marking point during the rehearsal as to when to start walking. This could be when the bridesmaid in front of you gets halfway down the aisle, or to a certain seat. Most bridesmaids are told to walk slowly, with one foot coming in and almost stopping at the other before moving forward. Finally, remember to smile. You shouldn't be nervous, the focus is on the bride today.

One important thing to remember, once you get to your spot to stand: *don't lock your knees*. Keep your knees bent/relaxed to avoid aggravating a fainting spell.

Next the music will change again and the wedding guests will stand, signifying the entrance of the bride. Wedding party members should be well versed on their responsibilities so it shouldn't be a question of who fluffs the bride's train, who is holding the rings, or when to pass your flowers to the person behind you if an extra hand is needed.

This is your time to enjoy the ceremony and be the witness to the joining of the couple you are representing.

Once the ceremony is done, the bride and groom leave down the aisle followed by the wedding party. They may all then re-enter the wedding site for pictures while the guests begin their route to the reception.

At this point, pictures taken include the bride and the groom, the wedding party, and any family members or friends of the couple's choice. This usually takes about thirty minutes.

THE RECEPTION

Once the picture taking is done, everyone heads over to the reception. Sometimes the guests are asked to wait outside until the wedding party arrives so they can create a welcome line for the guests. This will be part of your duties as a bridal party member if this is done. The usual procession of a receiving line is as follows: First - the parents of the groom; second - the parents of the bride; third - the bride and groom; and then forth - the members of the wedding party. Most of the guests you probably won't know, so as people come by, shake their hand. You can introduce yourself, telling how you know the couple, or ask the guest how he/she knows the couple and tell them you are happy they could make it.

Instead of a receiving line you may be asked at this point to greet guests at the guest registry or the gift table. For the guest registry you simply stand by the registry book, greet guests, and make sure they have a pen to sign the book. For the gift table, simply stand and take wedding gifts from the guests as they arrive.

Once everyone is inside the reception, you may be free to mingle or you may be requested for more pictures. Usually you can mingle, and get something to drink and eat while the bride and groom meet with all of the guests. If this is a sit-down dinner you will be reserved a table and you are welcome to sit and enjoy your meal if you are not needed for any other activities. The reception focuses more on the bride and groom than the wedding party.

Sometimes the bridesmaids use their flower bouquet to adorn the gift table or wedding cake table. Take your cue from the bride.

If the bride and groom have music and dancing at the wedding the first dance is reserved for them. Then the second dance is reserved for the bride to dance with her father while the groom dances with his mother. The third dance is for the couple to dance with their in-laws. At this point, you are welcome to join the floor with a dance partner.

Some couples will also perform the "money dance" at this time. The "money dance" is where the guests pay to dance with either the bride or the groom. Guests can give a dollar or more for a short dance until someone cuts in. This is designed to give the bride and groom money to start their new life together.

The next event you may be involved in is the cutting of the cake. Photographers like to have the wedding party gather around the cake for pictures before it is dismembered. At this time you may also participate in what is known as a "ring pull." If it is done it usually takes the place of the throwing of the bride's bouquet.

During a "ring pull," all single women are asked to gather around the bride's wedding cake. Each woman is asked to hold onto one of the ribbons extending from the cake through the icing. On the count of three all the women in unison pull on their ribbon. The ribbons are attached to little silver trinkets hidden in the cake. The one who pulls out the ring is the one expected to marry next. All the trinkets have a certain meaning (e.g. the horseshoe means luck and the dove means peace) so ask the bride what your trinket means if you are not sure.

If the ring pull is not performed the next event that may require your participation is the bouquet toss. Again, this is where all the single women are asked to gather in a certain part of the room. The bride then turns her back and throws her bouquet into the air. The woman who catches it is believed to be the next to marry.

For the men, the next activity that may require your participation is the garter toss. Before this activity, the groom usually has the bride sit in a chair or stand while he takes the garter that she has been wearing during the ceremony from her leg, usually worn mid-thigh.

The groom then asks all single men to gather around. The groom then stands backwards and tosses or flings the garter back. The male to catch the garter is believed to be the next to marry. Sometimes there is a belief that the couple who catch the bouquet and the garter will marry each other. Pictures of the two are usually taken at this point.

Soon before the couple plans to depart they may leave the reception to change into clothes for departure on their honeymoon. At this point, you may be requested to hand out to guests little packets of birdseed or (growing more popular) bubble blowers to shower the newly married couple as they disembark.

You may also be asked to bring the car of the newlyweds around to the front entrance for them and direct guests to the outside for the nearing departure.

Soon the newlyweds will appear and race to their car as guests shower them with bubbles or seed, and then wish them well as they depart for their honeymoon.

Chapter VIII
After the wedding

⸺⟫⋅◉⋅⟪⸺

*A*fter the couple leaves for their honeymoon, you may have a few extra duties to do. It is not your responsibility to clean up the reception, but a few things can be helpful.

A lot of guests bring their gifts to the wedding reception. You can help by loading the gifts into the cars of the bride and groom's family members or by helping to transport the gifts yourself.

Also, you can help to make sure that the bride's dress and other belongings are taken care of by a relative or you may have been requested to take them yourself. They need to be kept until she returns from her honeymoon.

The newlyweds also need to have the top layer of the bridal cake wrapped securely and stored in a freezer until they return. Then they can move it into their freezer to be thawed out and eaten on their one-year anniversary.

One popular idea at receptions is to give guests disposable cameras to take candid shots during the reception. If this was done, you can offer to collect the cameras and drop them at a local photo processing store for the newlyweds to pick up upon their return.

If you know there are out-of-town guests you can also make yourself available to take them to the airport that day or the next if you are available.

In a final note, the groomsmen need to make sure their tuxedo is returned. For bridesmaids, the dress is yours to keep to wear to other formal occasions.

Phew you did it! Pat yourself on the back at this time, you did a job well done!

THE END

ABOUT THE AUTHOR:

This book was brought on by the author's attendance as a bridesmaid in over a dozen weddings. Due to her extensive wedding experience people were constantly asking about bridal duties and expectations. This book is designed to help answer those questions for those she may not have direct contact with and help ease any anxiety. The author graduated from bridesmaid to bride in 1999 and lives happily with her husband and their two children. Since then, she has also enjoyed her work as the role of bridesmatron and wedding consultant in several weddings.

www.ingramcontent.com/pod-product-compliance
Lightning Source LLC
Chambersburg PA
CBHW020410290526
45785CB00005B/2495